# IS PREMARITAL SEX FORBIDDEN IN THE BIBLE?

# Is Premarital Sex Forbidden in the Bible?

SOLOMON THOMAS JACOB

# Contents

This book is dedicated to all single Christians, especially those who have struggled with the question of how to balance your love of God and commitment to Him against your hormones and inherent sexual desires.  Many of us suffer alone in silence because we do not find clear guidance.

Father God, I pray that you would guide the path this book takes, both my journey in writing it and the impact and response of those who read it.  I pray that Your will would be done in our lives, regardless of our biases, fears, hopes, and wishes on this subject.  Please help us to remember that the greatest commandment is to love You with all our heart, all our soul, and all our mind.  Please help us to remember that the second greatest commandment is to love our neighbors as ourselves.  Please help us to do both and please help us to remember both at all times that our sexuality occupies our thoughts, feelings, or actions.  In Jesus' name I pray, amen.

# Chapter 1

# Introduction

So, here's my dilemma. I was raised in a Christian household, in Christian churches. No matter where we lived, Sunday School, youth group, and church were constants growing up. Among other things, I was taught before puberty that sex was only for after marriage. These weren't hypocritical, fake people; they believed in what they said and their lives matched what they were saying (unlike many churches today). As a good boy, I simply accepted this as a fact of life. But as I entered puberty and my sexuality came alive, I wanted to know that since I've agreed to not have sex (since clearly, I wasn't married), what exactly should I do and not do when it came to my sexual feelings and females? Crickets. I wanted to do right, so I decided at the age of thirteen to ignore anything I heard "on the streets" about sex, girls, etc., and only listen to what I heard from church. But the most "concrete" answer I ever got was from a pastor who said, "keep everything buttoned up, zipped up, and fastened up and you'll be okay." That's technically not even true, aside from it also having no Biblical backing.

That left me living in a zone of confusion for decades, not really sure where the line should be but also with the messaging that "as the man I'm supposed to be the lead." Marry that with "if the blind lead the blind…" and yeah, not an encouraging prescription. Eventually, I got tired of the non-answers and determined that as a very well educated, multi-degreed professional, I should be able to figure this out on my own. So, Bible in hand, I began searching for the scriptures that say what I can and cannot do sexually. I figured I'd start with the scriptures that say I can't have sex and build a framework from there until I had a complete understanding of how I should live as a single Christian.

But I couldn't find them. From Genesis to Revelation, I tried. I used some of the popular verses people like to quote, even though they didn't really fit, and tried to create a framework to live by. But even if nobody else realized it (the verses didn't match the message), I knew, and I wasn't at peace with it.

(As an aside, I was taught to be very judgmental of people who engage in "sexual sin." This experience has made me a lot less so. While granted, many people follow sexual practices they believe to be sin, it is clear now that there is a lot less certainty than we have been taught and if Christians can't all agree on Sunday vs. Saturday worship or more esoteric things, I can't bring myself to have any negative feelings about different conclusions on sex, whether they are more conservative or more liberal than mine.)

Unless otherwise noted, I will use the New American Standard Bible (NASB) translation for quoted scriptures. Scriptures will be placed in italics.

# Chapter 2

# Sole Sufficiency
# of Scripture

The only source for knowing what is or is not sin is
the Bible.  Sin is, by definition, a deviation from
God's instruction for our lives.  And that instruction is,
specifically and exclusively, the Bible.

II Timothy 3:16,17

> *All Scripture is inspired by God and beneficial
> for teaching, for rebuke, for correction, for training
> in righteousness; so that the man or woman of God
> may be fully capable, equipped for every good work.*

Deuteronomy 4:2

> *You shall not add to the word which I am com-
> manding you, nor take away from it, so that you
> may keep the commandments of the Lord your God
> which I am commanding you.*

Proverbs 30:6

> *Do not add to His words Or He will rebuke you,
> and you will be proved a liar.*

A detail often missed is that Eve (and presumably Adam) is guilty of doing this in the Garden of Eden. In Genesis 2:16,17 God gives Adam the following command:

> *The Lord God commanded the man, saying, "From any tree of the garden you may freely eat; but from the tree of the knowledge of good and evil you shall not eat, for on the day that you eat from it you will certainly die."*

God then creates Eve. In Genesis 3:1-3, the serpent tempts Eve by challenging this command:

> *Now the serpent was more cunning than any animal of the field which the Lord God had made. And he said to the woman, "Has God really said, 'You shall not eat from any tree of the garden'?" The woman said to the serpent, "From the fruit of the trees of the garden we may eat; but from the fruit of the tree which is in the middle of the garden, God has said, 'You shall not eat from it or touch it, or you will die.'"*

What Eve said does not match what God said. She added an additional commandment to not touch the fruit. God never said that. It is not clear if she is the one who added this additional instruction or if it was Adam. Adam is present (indicated in verse 6) and he does not correct her, so both are complicit in changing the commandment. (I Timothy 2:13,15 also indicates that Eve was deceived while Adam was not.) Deuteronomy 4:2 perhaps indicates that adding to or subtracting from God's commandments will lead to failure to follow His commandments. It is worth noting that moments after Adam and Eve added to God's commandment, they went on to break His actual commandment.

I kind of wonder if it's a temptation to add to scripture to "make it extra hard and make sure we're doing it." That would come from a place of arrogance that says we know better than God. It is of course foolish because we do not know better than God. It is also dangerous because He has a reason for everything He says and if we try to supersede it, we may bypass protections He put in place for our benefit. Worse, it may come from a place of pride of wanting to look even holier by doing more than what God said.

Are we as a church guilty of violating Deuteronomy 4:2 and Proverbs 30:6 in the area of sexual immorality?

Such a question is automatically unacceptable because it violates the teaching of men and women of authority in the church. However, that is irrelevant. The question is what does the Word of God say? That is the sole authority.

We are comfortable with what we have been taught, no matter what that actually is. But Jesus is clear that we cannot replace the Word of God with the teachings of humans, not even if those humans are leaders in the church.

Mark 7:6-9

> *But He said to them, "Rightly did Isaiah prophesy about you hypocrites, as it is written: 'This people*

*honors Me with their lips, But their heart is far away from Me. And in vain do they worship Me, Teaching as doctrines the commandments of men.' Neglecting the commandment of God, you hold to the tradition of men." He was also saying to them, "You are experts at setting aside the commandment of God in order to keep your tradition.*

It is also important to establish that I am making a central tenant the belief that it was God's intention that His commandments were given in a way that they can be understood.

I Corinthians 14:7-11,33

*Yet even lifeless instruments, whether flute or harp, in producing a sound, if they do not produce a distinction in the tones, how will it be known what is played on the flute or on the harp? For if the trumpet produces an indistinct sound, who will prepare himself for battle? So you too, unless you produce intelligible speech by the tongue, how will it be known what is spoken? For you will just be talking to the air. There are, perhaps, a great many kinds of languages in the world, and none is incapable of meaning. So if I do not know the meaning of the language, I will be unintelligible to the one who speaks, and the one who speaks will be unintelligible to me...for God is not a God of confusion, but of peace.*

Yes, the Bible is translated into many languages and the American English I speak today is not the Hebrew, Aramaic, or Greek in which its various books were written.  I use the New American Standard Bible because it is widely recognized as one of the most accurate translations from those original texts.  We, of course, can mistranslate, as anyone who has taken a foreign language class in school knows.  But I believe that as originally written, the meaning / intent of every commandment was clearly understood.  Thus, with the possible exception of needing to do some language research to understand word translations, idioms, and other subtleties of ancient languages, any Biblical command that significantly impacts life choices must be clear enough for an average individual to understand it without assistance.  If it is not, there is a possibility that the reader (or person providing assistance) is inventing a command that is not actually there.

10   ~   SOLOMON THOMAS JACOB

## Chapter 3

# Other Areas of Theological Disagreement

That being said, Christians do not always agree on what is in the Bible. There are many issues where intelligent, spirit-filled, God-fearing Christians read the same Bible and reach drastically different conclusions about what God has said. Without digressing to delve deeply into the details of any of these, I will briefly highlight a few areas where there has been division within the Church over the past several centuries:

### Creation

Many are aware that for centuries there have been debates of creation versus evolution to explain how the universe and humanity came to be. But ignoring all non-biblical discussion, if one uses only scripture, aside from any other input, there are still conflicting views as to how the universe came to be. Some of the more popular schools of thought include: (1) the young universe – based on counting all of the ages and durations in the Bible up to the point where there are established records of humanity, there is roughly 6,000 years, give or take a few hundred, between the creation of the universe and the present year; (2) day-age – based on II Peter 3:8, (*But do not let this one fact escape your notice, beloved, that with the Lord one day is like a thousand years, and a thousand years like one day*) the durations and ages listed in the Bible are viewed as fluid and can be expanded to match any claim for the age of the universe; (3) ruin-reconstruction (also known as gap) – based on an assumption; this idea places a gap between Genesis 1:1 and 1:2, suggesting that there was an initial creation eons ago (Genesis 1:1), but somehow that creation is devastated and a new creation takes place (beginning with 1:2), thereby allowing the 6,000 years of the young universe idea to occur starting at 1:2 and billions of years to transpire in the gap between 1:1 and 1:2.  There are easily found documented records, at least as recently as the mid-1980s, from sincere bible scholars within each of these (and other) camps, each convinced they are following what the Word of God literally says.

## Rapture

There are also at least three different camps surrounding the rapture – the event when Jesus returns to gather all Christians to heaven.  Some believe the rapture is pre-tribulation, that is the rapture is the event that immediately precedes the 7-year period of chaos and judgment in the world. This is depicted in the *Left Behind* series of movies and books. Others believe the rapture is mid-tribulation, that it occurs at the 3.5-year mark of the tribulation. Others believe the rapture is post-tribulation and does not occur until immediately after the tribulation and just before the Battle of Armageddon. (Of course, there are also those who do not believe in the existence of the rapture or tribulation at all.)

## Saturday vs. Sunday Worship

Day of worship is also an area of differing beliefs. Most Christian denominations worship primarily on Sunday, in honor of the day Jesus rose from the dead. However, others, most notably the Seventh Day Adventists, worship on Saturday as a commitment to keep the Sabbath. (A few Christians are not even aware that the Sabbath is Saturday, not Sunday.) It is worth noting that since the 14$^{th}$ century, Ethiopian Christians observe a two-day Sabbath, covering both Saturday and Sunday. Many non-denominational or less rigid denominational churches hold services on whatever days or times are convenient for their membership. Those who do not worship on Saturday generally cite Colossians 2:16-17 as evidence that the Sabbath is not binding for Christians. Those who do worship on Saturday cite Exodus 20:8-11 and Deuteronomy 5:12-15.

## Curse of Ham and Slavery

One of the justifications used to justify slavery and racism in general is the curse of Ham.  The basis is Genesis 9:20-27, which surrounds Noah becoming drunk and the actions of his offspring.  Starting in the late 1700s American pastors preached that African slavery was justified by the curse of Ham.  However, it is obvious from reading Genesis 9 that there is no curse of Ham.  Ham was never cursed.  His son, Canaan, was cursed, but African people are not descended from Canaan.  Canaan was the father of the Canaanites and other people groups in the Bible including the Amorites, Girgashites, Hittites, Hivites, Jebusites, Sidonians, Arkites, Sinites, Arvadites, Zemarites, Hamathites, and the Perizzites.  The region his descendants settled include modern day Israel, Palestine, Lebanon, Syria, and Jordan and genetic testing has confirmed that the people of Lebanon are descended from the historic Canaanites. (By comparison, African peoples were descended from other sons of Ham – Cush, Mizraim, and Phut.)

Genesis 9:24-27

> *When Noah awoke from his wine, he knew what his youngest son had done to him. So he said, "Cursed be Canaan; A servant of servants He shall be to his brothers." He also said, "Blessed be the Lord, The God of Shem; And may Canaan be his servant. May God enlarge Japheth, And may he live in the tents of Shem; And may Canaan be his servant."*

While there may still be Christians today who promote the curse of Ham, it is literally a case of heresy – at best poor reading comprehension and at worst an intentional twisting of scripture. The Southern Baptist denomination (there are presently 14 major Baptist denominations) was formed in 1845 when it split from what was then mainline Baptism over the issue of whether slaveowners should be allowed to be appointed as missionaries. (The Home Mission Society had issued a statement saying that a person could not be a missionary and keep his slaves as property and the Southern Baptists refused to comply.) By comparison, other denominations directly opposed or challenged slavery, including the Quakers, Wesleyan Methodist Church, African Methodist Episcopal Church, American Baptist Free Mission Society.

These are just a few of the areas where Christians who believe the Bible is the sole Word of God still disagree over what it says. In some of these areas, many of us hold very clear views to the point where we are certain the other viewpoints are absolutely wrong. Others may be grayer, where it is difficult to tell who is right and who is wrong. Maybe in some cases it may look like everybody is right, or everybody is wrong. And we can see that there can be devastating consequences when the wrong thing is believed to be right.

# Chapter 4

# Unintentional Sin

S o, it is clear that even if we are looking to the Bible, it is possible to come away with the wrong idea. What if we think we are doing the right thing but are not? What if we're just doing what we were taught in a sermon? Ultimately, just because a pastor said it is not good enough. And if you get it wrong, even if you never knew it was wrong, you are still in sin. Leviticus 5:17 applies:

> *Now if a person sins and does any of the things which the Lord has commanded not to be done, though he was unaware, he is still guilty and shall bear his punishment.*

Job took this seriously and in Job 1:5 it can be seen that Job would regularly offer burnt offerings just in case one of his sons might have sinned and cursed God in their hearts, something Job would inherently be unaware of had it occurred.

Numbers 15:22-31 goes into more detail as to how Israel was to address unintentional sin.

*'But when you unintentionally do wrong and fail to comply with all these commandments which the Lord has spoken to Moses, that is, all that the Lord has commanded you through Moses from the day that the Lord gave commandments and onward, throughout your generations, then it shall be, if it is done unintentionally, without the knowledge of the congregation, that all the congregation shall offer one bull as a burnt offering, as a soothing aroma to the Lord, with its grain offering and its drink offering, according to the ordinance, and one male goat as a sin offering. Then the priest shall make atonement for all the congregation of the sons of Israel, and they will be forgiven; for it was an unintentional wrong, and they have brought their offering, an offering by fire to the Lord, and their sin offering before the Lord, for their unintentional wrong. So all the congregation of the sons of Israel will be forgiven, as well as the stranger who resides among them, for guilt was attributed to all the people through an unintentional wrong. 'Also, if one person sins unintentionally, then he shall offer a one-year-old female goat as a sin offering. And the priest shall make atonement before the Lord for the person who goes astray by an unintentional sin, making atonement for him so that he may be forgiven. You shall have one law for the native among the sons of Israel and for the*

*stranger who resides among them, for one who does anything wrong unintentionally. But the person who does wrong defiantly, whether he is a native or a stranger, that one is blaspheming the Lord; and that person shall be cut off from among his people. Since he has despised the word of the Lord and has broken His commandment, that person shall be completely cut off; his guilt will be on him.'*

Philippians 2:12,1

*So then, my beloved, just as you have always obeyed, not as in my presence only, but now much more in my absence, work out your own salvation with fear and trembling; for it is God who is at work in you, both to desire and to work for His good pleasure.*

# Chapter 5

# Commonly Cited Scriptures

I have seen a handful of scriptures commonly cited as justification when pastors and bible study leaders teach that Christians should remain virgins (or abstinent) until marriage.

### I Corinthians 6:18

This is one of the most commonly cited scriptures when it comes to singles and sex, often quoted as written in the King James Version:

> *Flee fornication. Every sin that a man doeth is without the body; but he that committeth fornication sinneth against his own body.*

When I was younger, I was taught an incorrect definition of the word fornication, at least as it appears in the KJV Bible. I was taught that fornication meant having sex with someone you are not married to. It was straightforward, black and white, and a clear guideline

I could follow. But that is not what the Bible actually says and some argue that the word fornication should not even appear in the Bible because it's not what Paul wrote. In fact, it does not appear at all in Bible translations known for their accuracy in translating the original text, such as the NIV and NASB. The Greek word that the KJV translates as "fornication" is the word pornea, which is translated more accurately (at least for modern English as opposed to the form of English spoken in the 1600s when the KJV was published) in the NIV and the NASB's rendition of I Corinthians 6:18:

*Flee sexual immorality. Every other sin that a person commits is outside the body, but the sexually immoral person sins against his own body.*

The command to flee from sexual immorality does not create any new restrictions or commandments. Anything that could constitute "sexual immorality" must have by definition already been restricted in a previously established commandment. Thus, it is clear that I Corinthians 6:18 only emphasizes what has already been commanded.

So, what, then is sexual immorality? Clearly it must be something that is sexual AND something that is immoral. Admittedly, we could split hairs on what is or is not sexual (and it would distract from the real issue to do so), but the key is understanding what is immoral. The only Christian definition for morality is the Word of God. In order for any act to be immoral, either the act itself or the method of performing the act must in some way be forbidden in the Bible. Ultimately, if something is immoral, it doesn't matter whether it is sexual or not. Any immorality is still sin.

But the bottom line is that I Corinthians 6:18 does not introduce a commandment to unmarried persons to abstain from sex. If such a commandment exists in the Bible, it would be emphasized by this verse, but it is not found in this verse.

### I Corinthians 7:1,2

*Now concerning the things about which you wrote, it is good for a man not to touch a woman. But because of sexual immoralities, each man is to have his own wife, and each woman is to have her own husband.*

This is another verse in the same book that is often cited. It is often read to mean that it is a sin for a man to touch a woman. Some will define touch as sexual intercourse, while others define it as even casual touch, like shaking hands. (There is an extremist faction in the arena of Christian "dating" that holds that Christians who are "courting" – they don't allow for dating – should not even hold hands.) Is that what Paul is saying? Does he really mean that as a man, my skin should never come into physical contact with the skin of a female unless she is my wife? Or is it okay if it is a casual touch, but not okay if it is sensual?

A mentor encouraged me to study the Greek in this verse, starting with the word translated as touch. I am not an expert in languages. So, I'm limited here to what

I can do with Google and with a Bible I own that has a limited Hebrew/Greek dictionary and lexicon.

The quality of Greek translation appears slightly inconsistent (or rather my grasp of Greek is insufficient). In one Bible with select Greek translations, touch in I Corinthians 7:1 is haptomai, which means touch, or to attach oneself to. Its lexicon describes haptomai as such handling of an object as to exert a modifying influence upon it or upon oneself.

The online interlinear Bible at biblehub.com indicates the Greek word used for touch in I Corinthians 7:1 is haptesthai and indicates it is also used in Luke 6:19 – "And all the multitude were trying to touch Him, for power was coming from Him and healing them all." This interlinear Bible indicates there are a large number of variations on the Greek words that are all translated as touch in the NASB. (I think this is a subtlety of the Greek language that is going over my head and not actual differences in the words.)

Both Bibles' Greek definitions suggest that in the case of I Corinthians 7:1, this is definitely an intentional touch that has meaning, not an accidental touch. It is not limited to sexual touch, however. While sexual touch would be included, any touch that creates a change – whether positive or negative – falls within the definition. So, there aren't really any surprises here. Touch means touch.

Most of the rest of the verse is similarly straightforward, but there are a couple of surprises.

The main surprise was the words used for woman and wife. In verse one, for the phrase, *"it is good for a man not to touch a woman,"* the Greek word gynaikos is used. In verse two, for the phrase, *"each man is to have his own wife,"* the Greek word gynaika is used. These are the same word, with the difference being that gynaikos (7:1) is in the Genitive Singular Feminine case and gynaika (7:2) is in the Accusative Singular Feminine case. From Wikipedia:

"In grammar, the genitive case is the grammatical case that marks a word, usually a noun, as modifying another word, also usually a noun—thus indicating an attributive relationship of one noun to the other noun...Genitive construction includes the genitive case, but is a broader category. Placing a modifying noun in the genitive case is one way of indicating that it is related to a head noun, in a genitive construction.

"The accusative case of a noun is the grammatical case used to mark the direct object of a transitive verb...In the English language, the only words that occur in the accusative case are pronouns: 'me,' 'him,' 'her,' 'us,' and 'them'...The accusative case is used in many languages for the objects of (some or all) prepositions. It is usually combined with the nominative case (for example in Latin)."

Unless you're a grammar buff, this is irrelevant and arguably boring. Bottom line, one Greek word is used in both verses, in one place translated into English as woman and another time as wife. This word is used 221 times in the New Testament, translated 129 times as woman and 92 times as wife (in the KJV), as reported in https://www.blueletterbible.org/lexicon/g1135/nasb20/mgnt/0-4/#lexResults. This website did not indicate if the same ratio was present in the New American Standard Bible (NASB), New International Version (NIV), or other translations. My grasp of language is not sufficient to determine whether there was clear reason to translate this Greek word as woman in some verses and as wife in others.

There is another place where woman occurs – *"each woman is to have her own husband."* In this case, the phrase "each woman" in Greek is the word hekastē, a nominative singular feminine adjective. It parallels the use of man in the phrase, *"each man is to have his own wife,"* where "each man" in Greek is hekastos, a nominative singular masculine adjective. This is straightforward, with the only uncertainty being the assignment of wife or woman to gynaikos/gynaika. With no additional means to make a choice as to whether the word should have been translated as wife or as woman, this leads to four possible translations of this verse:

1. *Now concerning the things about which you wrote, it is good for a man not to touch a*

**woman**. *But because of sexual immoralities, each man is to have his own **wife**, and each woman is to have her own husband.*

2. *Now concerning the things about which you wrote, it is good for a man not to touch a **wife**. But because of sexual immoralities, each man is to have his own **wife**, and each woman is to have her own husband.*

3. *Now concerning the things about which you wrote, it is good for a man not to touch a **woman**. But because of sexual immoralities, each man is to have his own **woman**, and each woman is to have her own husband.*

4. *Now concerning the things about which you wrote, it is good for a man not to touch a **wife**. But because of sexual immoralities, each man is to have his own **woman**, and each woman is to have her own husband.*

If there was a relevant difference in meaning between these verses the translation of gynaikos/gynaika would be important to resolve. However, there is no difference relevant to the current question. The issue at hand is we are looking for a passage that would convey a commandment for single persons to abstain from sex. Whether gynaikos/gynaika is best translated as woman or wife does not change the presence or absence of such a commandment. It may matter for other reasons, but not for this question. It is also worth noting that all translations I have seen used the first option, using woman in the first instance and wife in the second. I will assume (without actual knowledge to confirm) that is the correct translation.

The next word of interest is "good." Paul used good four times in this chapter (7:1, 7:8, and twice in 7:26), with the Greek word being kaylos. Kaylos is used 102 times in the New Testament and is translated in the KJV as good (83x), better (7x), honest (5x), meet (2x), goodly (2x), or miscellaneous (3x). Good is used in this chapter to reflect Paul's preferences, but is not used to convey a command. In verse 8 he indicates that it is good for the unmarried and widows to remain as he is and in verse 26, he says it is good for a man to remain as he is. "Good" does not equal "must" or "shall."

And this is where the logic error emerges that causes so many Christians to have difficulty with this verse and where some have been led to impose incredibly extreme restrictions in their dating lives, but those reactions indicate a fundamental misunderstanding of both the passage and language in general.

Notice the wording carefully. *"It is good for a man not to touch a woman,"* is a radically different statement from, "a man shall not touch a woman." The second statement is a command to not touch a woman. If Paul had said that, then there would be cause for substantial restrictions in male-female interaction (not just sexual). But he made no such command. He did issue a value judgment that it is good for men to not touch women (or possibly wives). But this does not imply that it is bad for men to touch women. Drawing such a conclusion is a reading comprehension error, specifically the one known as Denying the Antecedent (a form of if-then fallacy). It is possible – and frequent – for two opposite activities to both be good. For instance, it is good to rest. It is also good to exercise. It is good to sleep. It is also good to be awake. It is good to be analytical and think things through. It is also good to be emotional and feel things through. Seemingly opposites, but all are good.

Denying the Antecedent is a formal fallacy that infers the inverse from the original statement. It takes the form of, "If P, then Q. Therefore, if not P, then not Q." What happens is people (in their minds) make the leap to read into the passage, saying in their minds, "if a man does not touch a woman then good occurs," therefore "if a man does touch a woman then not good (sin) occurs."

$$P = \text{man does not touch a woman}$$
$$Q = \text{good occurs}$$
$$\text{Not } P = \text{man does touch a woman}$$
$$\text{Not } Q = \text{not good (sin) occurs}$$

It is a logic error to conclude that if it is "good" to do a specific thing then it is "bad" to do the opposite of that thing. When you make this mistake, you have actually added words to scripture that were never there. You have replaced the Word of God with your own words. For a real-world example of how this is not so, let's look at how a Christian is supposed to treat others. Let's say someone approaches a Christian with love (P). The result is the Christian responds with love (Q). (If you approach a Christian in love, then he/she will react in love.) But, let's say someone approaches a Christian with hate (not P). The Christian (assuming the Christian is not sinning) will still respond with love (Q, which is not "not Q").

We must be very careful to not construct logical fallacies or in any other way add things to scripture when we read the Bible. When you add to a passage, you inherently change its meaning. We must deal ONLY with what is written, with no additions or assumptions. If we believe God could not write exactly what He meant, then we put ourselves in the position of speaking for God, adding our intelligence where His has fallen short.

As a footnote to this discussion, it is worth considering the other surprise I uncovered, whether verse one is misinterpreted as traditionally understood, and whether other potential meanings affect the discussion.

> *Now concerning the things about which you wrote, it is good for a man not to touch a woman.*

What are the "things about which you wrote"? We know that I Corinthians is a letter to the church at Corinth in response to messages they sent to Paul. Is the phrase, "it is good for a man not to touch a woman," Paul's statement? Or was it the "things" about which the church at Corinth wrote to Paul? Theologians debate this, but technically, the phrasing in question could extend all the way to verse 5. (The use of "I" in verse 6 would seemingly indicate that verse and after is clearly part of Paul's response, technically leaving only verses 1 and 5 in question, with most only questioning verse 1.)

So, who said, "it is good for a man not to touch a woman"? There are three possibilities: perhaps Paul said it; perhaps members of the church at Corinth said it to Paul; or perhaps a third party said it to members of the church at Corinth and those members are now asking Paul about it. Ultimately, it is a red herring (distraction) to my primary question – whether premarital sex is forbidden in the Bible. The church has changed opinions in the past regarding who is saying what in this verse and may well do so again. However, the highest authority can be tied to the phrase if Paul is the one who spoke it. (If someone else said it, then Paul must either agree, in which case it's as if he said it, or Paul must disagree, in which case the passage can be discarded as non-binding.) Consequently, I previously addressed these verses as if the words (and ideas) were coming from Paul. And ultimately, based on that – the most stringent possible interpretation – I Corinthians 7:1.2 does not contain a prohibition of premarital sex.

<u>I Corinthians 7:8,9</u>
> *But I say to the unmarried and to widows that it is good for them if they remain even as I. But if they do*

*not have self-control, let them marry; for it is better to marry than to burn with passion.*

For the sake of clarity, I do think it important to look up several of the Greek words in this verse: unmarried, widows, self-control, and burn.

<u>Unmarried</u>
https://biblehub.com/greek/agamois_22.htm
https://www.studylight.org/lexicons/eng/greek/22.html

Definition
**1. unmarried, unwedded, single**

Interestingly, the definition given for agamois is simply unmarried.  There is, unfortunately, a lack of clarity as to whether unmarried/unwedded means never married, or if it means formerly married but now not.  The widest applicability will be to assume it includes all whose current martial status does not equal married.  However, doing so might erroneously include those who are not allowed to get married again (e.g., Matthew 5:32, Matthew 19:9, Luke 16:18, Mark 10:11,12).

<u>Widows</u>
https://biblehub.com/greek/che_rais_5503.htm
https://www.studylight.org/lexicons/eng/greek/5503.html

Definition

1. a widow
2. metaph. a city stripped of its inhabitants and riches is represented under the figure of a widow

As per the definition, this is specifically referring to formerly married women whose husbands have died. The Greek for widow does not include the English word widower.  And it is unclear if a widower is captured in the word unmarried.

Self-Control

https://biblehub.com/greek/1467.htm

https://www.studylight.org/lexicons/eng/greek/1467.html

Definition

1. to be self-controlled, continent
2. to exhibit self-government, conduct, one's self temperately
3. in a figure drawn from athletes, who in preparing themselves for the games abstained from unwholesome food, wine, and sexual indulgence

Burn

https://biblehub.com/greek/purousthai_4448.htm

https://www.studylight.org/lexicons/eng/greek/4448.html

Definition
1. to burn with fire, to set on fire, kindle
    a. to be on fire, to burn
        i. to be incensed, indignant
    b. make to glow
        i. full of fire, fiery, ignited
    c. of darts filled with inflammable substances and set on fire
        i. melted by fire and purged of dross

Paul does appear to be saying to women whose husbands have died and to both genders who are not married (and presumably, but not definitively, are eligible for marriage) and who do not wish to restrain their sexual desire that they should marry, because it is better to be married than to be on fire (presumably, but not definitively, referencing sexual desire with no outlet). But is this a command? No, it is not. Though it does recognize the obvious.

Virtually any person who is not married and has an active sex drive will experience what could be described as "burning," whether that person is abstinent or engaging in sex. Sexual intercourse requires two people. A single individual is only one person. So, whether one chooses to abstain or is simply unable to find a suitable person for sex, most single persons could be described as at times burning with sexual desire. It may well be inevitable for all except perhaps the most popular/desirable (assuming no lies/manipulation/deceit or other forbidden practices are used to gain sex). As a general rule, this "burning" should not happen for a married person. I Corinthians 7:3-5 (literally just a few words before the ones we are studying here) is clear that husband and wife are not to deny sex to each other:

> *The husband must fulfill his duty to his wife, and likewise the wife also to her husband. The wife does not have authority over her own body, but the husband does; and likewise the husband also does not have authority over his own body, but the wife does. Stop depriving one another, except by agreement for a time so that you may devote yourselves to prayer, and come together again so that Satan will not tempt you because of your lack of self-control.*

In a proper marriage, neither husband nor wife should experience the kind of burning that is simply part of life for a typical single person. (Paul considered himself to not be typical in this manner and presumably had no sexual desire.) However, nowhere in verses 8 and 9 is any kind of command that prohibits sexual intercourse prior to marriage. If it exists in the Bible, it is not here. All that is here is an extremely sensible recommendation on how to avoid sexual frustration.

It is important to keep in mind that there was a school of thought in Corinth at the time that a person was spiritually superior if they did not get married and did not have sex. In such a community, even admitting to being horny would be a sign of weakness. And doing anything like satisfying sexual desire with a spouse would show you to be a "lesser" person. This runs entirely opposite to God's original command in Genesis 1:28 to be fruitful and multiply and the directive for men to get married in Genesis 2:24. It is most likely that Paul was focused on debunking this false teaching in much of I Corinthians 7.

It is obvious and must be reiterated that marriage is the goal, regardless of where one stands on premarital sex. The only exception is those who use singleness to focus entirely on 24/7 service to God. Such a person would literally have no time to spare on things like sex. The best modern-day metaphor would be the missionary whose full dedication is equivalent to that of an extreme workaholic.

### I Corinthians 7:36-38

> *But if anyone thinks that he is acting dishonorably toward his virgin, if she is past her youth and it ought to be so, let him do what he wishes, he is not sinning; let them marry. But the one who stands firm in his heart, if he is not under constraint, but has authority over his own will, and has decided this in his own heart, to keep his own virgin, he will do well. So*

*then, both the one who gives his own virgin in mar-
riage does well, and the one who does not give her in
marriage will do better.*

Like with other verses, before jumping in, we should
check several Greek words to be sure that nothing is
being lost in translation.  I will start with the following:
dishonorably, virgin, past her youth, keep:

Dishonorably
https://biblehub.com/greek/asche_mon-
ein_807.htm
https://biblehub.com/greek/807.htm
https://www.studylight.org/lexicons/eng/greek/
807.html

Definition
1. To behave improperly, to act unbecomingly
2. To act unbecomingly

Acting dishonorably is pretty straightforward.  This
would be someone who feels like he is doing the wrong
thing, or something not in her best interests.

<u>Virgin</u>
https://biblehub.com/greek/strongs_3933.htm
https://www.studylight.org/lexicons/eng/greek/
3933.html

Definition
1. a virgin
    a. a marriageable maiden
    b. a woman who has never had sexual in-
       tercourse with a man
    c. one's marriageable daughter
2. a man who has abstained from all uncleanness and whoredom attendant on idolatry,
   and so has kept his chastity
    a. one who has never had intercourse with
       women

<u>Past her youth</u>
https://biblehub.com/greek/5230.htm
https://www.studylight.org/lexicons/eng/greek/
5230.html

Definition
1. beyond the "acme", i.e. figuratively (of a
   daughter) past the bloom (prime) of youth
2. From huper and the base of akmen; beyond
   the "acme", i.e. Figuratively (of a daughter)
   past the bloom (prime) of youth -- + pass the
   flower of (her) age.

3. beyond the bloom or prime of life
4. overripe, plump and ripe, (and so in a greater danger of defilement)
   a. of a virgin
5. The adjective describes a woman who has passed the prime of her youth—no longer at the opening bloom of maidenhood, yet still unmarried. The term therefore evokes the tension between the passing of time and the need to make a prudent decision about marriage.

It ought

https://biblehub.com/greek/opheilei_3784.htm
https://biblehub.com/greek/strongs_3784.htm
https://biblehub.com/greek/3784.htm

Definition
1. To owe, to be indebted, to be obligated
2. to owe (finacially)
3. (figuratively) to be under obligation, indebted (ought, must, should)
4. (morally) to fail in duty
5. refers to being morally obligated (or legally required) to meet an obligation, i.e. to pay off a legitimate debt
6. originally belonged to the legal sphere; it expressed initially one's legal and economic, and then later one's moral, duties and re-

sponsibilities to the gods and to men, or to their sacrosanct regulations. . . . opheílō expresses human and ethical responsibility in the NT

7. to owe
    a. to owe money, be in debt for
        i. that which is due, the debt
8. metaph. the goodwill due

<u>Keep</u>

https://biblehub.com/greek/5083.htm
https://www.studylight.org/lexicons/eng/greek/5083.html

Definition
1. to attend to carefully, take care of
    a. to guard
    b. metaph. to keep, one in the state in which he is
    c. to observe
    d. to reserve: to undergo something
2. To keep, to guard, to observe, to watch over
3. to guard (from loss or injury)
4. (properly) by keeping the eye upon, i.e. to note (a prophecy)
5. (... figuratively) to fulfil a command
6. (by implication) to detain in custody
7. (... figuratively) to maintain
8. (by extension) to withhold for personal ends

## 9. (... figuratively) to keep unmarried

Paul just finished talking (in preceding verses) about the advantages a virgin has in pursuing the interests of the Lord. Now he appears to be considering a situation where a man who has possessive control over a virgin woman is deciding whether to allow her to marry or remain single. The driving motivation is either she should marry and further delay in marriage may be harmful, or she should remain single and he is protecting her by keeping her single. But who is this man? The NASB and the NIV translate this differently, in a way that alters the meaning:

> NASB: *"But if anyone thinks that he is acting dishonorably toward his virgin, if she is past her youth and it ought to be so, let him do what he wishes, he is not sinning; let them marry. But the one who stands firm in his heart, if he is not under constraint, but has authority over his own will, and has decided this in his own heart, to keep his own virgin, he will do well. So then, both the one who gives his own virgin in marriage does well, and the one who does not give her in marriage will do better."*

> NIV: *"If anyone is worried that he might not be acting honorably toward the virgin he is engaged to, and if his passions are too strong and he feels he ought to marry, he should do as he wants. He is not sin-*

*ning. They should get married. But the man who has settled the matter in his own mind, who is under no compulsion but has control over his own will, and who has made up his mind not to marry the virgin—this man also does the right thing. So then, he who marries the virgin does right, but he who does not marry her does better."*

I am inclined to go with the NASB translation. The Greek text of the verse does not include enough words to describe an engagement or the use of the phrase, "passions are too strong" (https://biblehub.com/text/1_corinthians/7-36.htm). Further, it makes no sense to be engaged to a woman and not marry her. It would be highly presumptive to call a woman "his virgin" unless he has already made a commitment to marry. Can you be engaged to a concubine??? This could maybe make sense if it was about a man and his concubine, choosing whether to elevate her to wife or not. But the Greek says nothing about any concubine relationship. Further, in the case of a fiancée interpretation, the choice presented would be to either (a) marry your virgin fiancée; or (b) keep her your fiancée and never marry her. From my understanding, betrothal in biblical times was much more serious than modern engagement. It was a commitment that was expected to be followed through on. It does not sound reasonable for Paul to be saying that the man who never marries his fiancée is doing better than the man who marries his fiancée.

However, this passage would make sense if the man in question were the woman's father (or perhaps an older brother or uncle in the case of the father being deceased). A man could talk about "my virgin" if he is talking about his own daughter. He also would be positioned in Hebrew society to make decisions about whether she marries or not. And, both in ancient and modern times, there are plenty of reasons for a father to be worried about his daughter's potential future husband. There is no end to stories of men mistreating their wives. "Keeping her safe" is entirely plausible. And so is "keeping her focused on the Lord," which appears to be more line with Paul's thinking about marriage throughout the chapter.

There are various details that could be discussed in the interpretation of these verses, but the bottom line is that this is only about the choice of whether to have a woman within a specific man's authority get married or not. There are no commandments in these verses about premarital sex (or sex at all).

### Genesis 2:24

> *For this reason a man shall leave his father and his mother, and be joined to his wife; and they shall become one flesh.*

While less often cited, this one is very appealing as it goes back to the creation of mankind. That being said, the introductory phrase, "For this reason" should first be understood before attempting to understand the rest of the passage. Whatever proceeds this introduction is the rationale for the statement in this verse. After reading the rest of chapter two it is evident that "this reason" is found in Genesis 2:18-23.

> *Then the Lord God said, "It is not good for the man to be alone; I will make him a helper suitable for him." And out of the ground the Lord God formed every animal of the field and every bird of the sky, and brought them to the man to see what he would call them; and whatever the man called a living creature, that was its name. The man gave names to all the livestock, and to the birds of the sky, and to every animal of the field, but for Adam there was not found a helper suitable for him. So the Lord God caused a deep sleep to fall upon the man, and he slept; then He took one of his ribs and closed up the flesh at that place. And the Lord God fashioned into a woman the rib which He had taken from the man, and brought her to the man. Then the man said, "At last this is bone of my bones, And flesh of my flesh; She shall be called 'woman,' Because she was taken out of man."*

In other words, man is not supposed to be alone; no animal is a substitute for human relation, not even a pet; God created woman as the proper companion for man. So that is the "why" behind Genesis 2:24.

So, what about the rest of Genesis 2:24? I looked up some of the key words in Hebrew just to make sure I'm not missing anything:

<u>Leave</u>

https://biblehub.com/hebrew/yaazov_5800.htm

https://www.studylight.org/lexicons/eng/hebrew/5800.html

Definition
1.   leave, loose, forsake
   a.   (Qal) to leave
      1.   to depart from, leave behind, leave, let alone
      2.   to leave, abandon, forsake, neglect, apostatize
      3.   to let loose, set free, let go, free
   b.   (Niphal)
      1.   to be left to
      2.   to be forsaken
   c.   (Pual) to be deserted
2.   to restore, repair
   a.   (Qal) to repair

<u>Joined</u>

https://biblehub.com/hebrew/vedavak_1692.htm

https://www.studylight.org/lexicons/eng/hebrew/1692.html

Definition

1.   to cling, stick, stay close, cleave, keep close, stick to, stick with, follow closely, join to, overtake, catch
   a.   (Qal)
      1.   to cling, cleave to
      2.   to stay with
   b.   (Pual) to be joined together
   c.   (Hiphil)
      1.   to cause to cleave to
      2.   to pursue closely
      3.   to overtake
   d.   (Hophal) to be made to cleave

One

https://biblehub.com/hebrew/echad_259.htm
https://www.studylight.org/lexicons/eng/hebrew/259.html

Definition

1.   one (number)
   a.   one (number)
   b.   each, every
   c.   a certain
   d.   an (indefinite article)
   e.   only, once, once for all
   f.   one...another, the one...the other, one after another, one by one
   g.   first

  h. eleven (in combination), eleventh (or-
   dinal)

<u>Flesh</u>

https://biblehub.com/hebrew/levasar_1320.htm

https://www.studylight.org/lexicons/eng/hebrew/
1320.html

Definition
1. flesh
  a. of the body
   1. of humans
   2. of animals
  b. the body itself
  c. male organ of generation (eu-
   phemism)
  d. kindred, blood-relations
  e. flesh as frail or erring (man against
   God)
  f. all living things
  g. animals
  h. mankind

I'm not seeing any hidden meanings here. The text
means what it says. Because woman (not animals/pets)
is the proper companion to man, a man is to separate
himself from his father and mother, bond to his wife,
and the two become almost literally a single entity. It

is repeated in I Corinthians 6:16 that the act of sex does make two people become one.

So, does the order of phrasing in Genesis 2:24 constitute a commandment?  If so, what kind?

> *For this reason a man shall leave his father and his mother, and be joined to his wife; and they shall become one flesh.*

Is this a mandatory sequence of steps or is it an accompanying result?  Is it a sequential commandment: step one – leave father and mother, step two – join to his wife, step three – become one flesh?  Or is it a result: because the only suiter helpable is a woman, the man steps out from his parents and marries a woman.  An inevitable consequence of a normal marriage is that the two become one?

It is clear that men are supposed to get married.  We are not intended to live single lives.  Even before sin entered the world, marriage was the plan.  Sin does impact this.  It results in many people not being suitable spouses.  It makes it difficult to find a spouse.  It makes many women afraid to place their trust and safety in a husband due to epidemic levels of domestic violence and sexual assault committed by men.  It encourages some, like Paul, to choose singleness as a means to focus more fully on serving God.  However, marriage is the original plan.  And it is clear that marriage is supposed to create a new household – with an intentional change in the relationship between a man and his parents.  And it is clear that sex is supposed to be present in marriage.   However, that is all this verse says.  It says nothing about any order of operations. In order to construct a required order, one must add words to the verse.

If an order of operations based on sentence structure was something we should assume from every scripture containing a series of actions, what would that imply about Romans 10:9?

> *that if you confess with your mouth Jesus as Lord, and believe in your heart that God raised Him from the dead, you will be saved;*

If a sequential order of operations was imposed on Romans 10:9 it would indicate that someone who believes first and confesses second would not be saved, because an assumed order of operations would require that you confess first and believe second.

Genesis 2:24 also says nothing about what happens outside of its three statements.  It does say that a man becomes one flesh with his wife.  It does not say a man may only become one flesh with his wife.  There may be (and are) restrictions elsewhere in the Bible, but those are not found here.

## Exodus 22:16, 17

> *If a man seduces a virgin who is not betrothed and sleeps with her, he must pay a dowry for her to be his wife.  If her father absolutely refuses to give her to him, he shall pay money equal to the dowry for virgins.*

It is worth pointing out that some theologians consider this passage irrelevant to the topic of whether or not premarital sex is forbidden. This group views this passage as related to the preceding verses on property rights and are about compensating the father for his economic loss (now that he can no longer gain the money that comes from having a virgin daughter get married). Others tie it to verse 19 (which issues a death penalty for having sex with an animal) and thus connect it to sex (despite verse 18 being entirely unrelated to sex). They then observe that the man seduced the woman, which means this is neither rape nor prostitution, and that this is a female virgin who is not engaged (and therefore not adultery). They then assume that because the man has to pay the father money (and marry her if the father permits it), then it must be a punishment and he has therefore sinned.

However, it is not at all clear that it is a punishment. As there is group of theologians who tie this verse to the economic loss, this may be no punishment at all. It may merely acknowledge that in Hebrew society, every father is entitled to a dowry for his daughters. It appears from context that the father of a virgin may (in all or some cases) receive a higher dowry than the father of a non-virgin.

It is also important to look at this type of sexual encounter. As previously noted, this is neither rape, nor prostitution, nor adultery. It is a fallacy, however, to assume that all sex that is neither rape, nor prostitution, nor adultery is the same. It may be seemingly minor, but is actually important to notice that this sex was achieved by seduction. This was not a case of mutual desire. The man had to do something to "seduce" the woman to agree. The Hebrew word translated as "seduce" in the NASB is pathah.

Seduce

https://biblehub.com/hebrew/strongs_6601.htm
https://www.studylight.org/lexicons/eng/hebrew/6601.html

Definition
1. to be spacious, be open, be wide
    a. (Qal) to be spacious or open or wide
    b. (Hiphil) to make spacious, make open
2. to be simple, entice, deceive, persuade
    a. (Qal)
        i. to be open-minded, be simple, be naive
        ii. to be enticed, be deceived
    b. (Niphal) to be deceived, be gullible
    c. (Piel)
    d. (Piel)
        i. to persuade, seduce
        ii. to deceive
    e. (Pual)
        i. to be persuaded

## ii. to be deceived

The "spacious" definition does not fit the context of this verse.  The other definitions include some form of "deception" as part of the definition.  This makes me think this is an instance of premarital sex where the woman would not have initially been interested in having sex, but the man told some kind of lie or manipulated her in some way that led to her giving consent.  This is a case of sexual deception, which is automatically sin because lies were involved, which were forbidden two chapters prior in Exodus 20:16.  Guilt is established on this basis (though the money paid to the father still may or may not be punishment), but cannot be extended to premarital sex where lies are not involved.

<u>Deuteronomy 22:20,21</u>
> *But if this charge is true, and they did not find the girl to have evidence of virginity, then they shall bring the girl out to the doorway of her father's house, and the men of her city shall stone her to death, because she has committed a disgraceful sin in Israel by playing the prostitute in her father's house; so you shall eliminate the evil from among you.*

However, I think this can be misinterpreted when read outside of proper context.  Deuteronomy 22:13-30 seem to be telling an integrated message:

*If any man takes a wife and goes in to her and then turns against her, and he charges her with shameful behavior and  publicly defames her, and says, 'I took this woman, but when I came near her, I did not find her to have evidence of virginity,' then the girl's father and her mother shall take and bring out the evidence of the girl's virginity to the elders of the city at the gate.  And the girl's father shall say to the elders, 'I gave my daughter to this man as a wife, but he turned against her; and behold, he has charged her with shameful behavior, saying, I did not find your daughter to have evidence of virginity.  But this is the evidence of my daughter's virginity.' And they shall spread out the garment before the elders of the city.  Then the elders of that city shall take the man and rebuke him, and they shall fine him a hundred shekels of silver and give it to the girl's father, because he publicly defamed a virgin of Israel. And she shall remain his wife; he is not allowed to divorce her all his days.  But if this charge is true, and they did not find the girl to have evidence of virginity, then they shall bring the girl out to the doorway of her father's house, and the men of her city shall stone her to death, because she has committed a disgraceful sin in Israel by playing the prostitute in her father's house; so you shall eliminate the evil from among you.  If a man is found sleeping with a married woman, then both of them shall die, the man who slept with the woman, and the woman; so you shall eliminate the evil from Israel.  If there is a girl who is a virgin betrothed to a man, and another man finds her in the city and sleeps with her, then you shall bring them both out to the gate of that city and you shall stone them to death: the girl, because she did not cry out for help though she was in the city, and the man, because he has violated his neighbor's wife. So you shall eliminate the evil from among you.  But if the man finds the girl who is betrothed in the field, and the man seizes her and rapes her, then only the man who raped her shall die.  And you are not to do anything to the girl; there is no sin in the girl worthy of death, for just as a man rises against his neighbor and murders him, so is this case.  When he found her in the field, the betrothed girl cried out, but there was no one to save her.  If a man finds a girl who is a virgin, who is not betrothed, and he seizes her and has sexual relations with her, and they are discovered, then the man who had sexual relations with her shall give the girl's father fifty shekels of silver, and she shall become his wife, because he has violated her; he is not allowed to divorce her all his days.  A man shall not take his father's wife in marriage, so that he does not uncover his father's garment.*

It is worth noting that there are several instances where death is called for in this passage:

| Event | Man Put to Death? | Woman Put to Death? |
| --- | --- | --- |
| Man marries a woman but discovers she is not a virgin (confirmed true) | No | Yes |
| Man found sleeping with a married woman | Yes | Yes |
| Man sleeps with an engaged virgin in the city | Yes | Yes |
| Man rapes an engaged young woman in the field | Yes | No |

In all cases, the woman is either married or engaged to one man, but has had sex with another. The first case is the subject of this discussion. In the second and third cases, both the man and the married woman consented to have sex, despite her being married to someone else, in violation of Leviticus 18:20. In the fourth case, the young woman (virgin or not – the word used, "naarah" specifically denotes a young woman by age as opposed to a virgin) is engaged to a different man, but she was raped and did not consent to the sex. So, the man is guilty, but the woman is not. The constant in cases 2-4 is that a willful intention to have sex with a woman who is promised to another man is a sin.

In case 1, the woman clearly lied. She became engaged and did not disclose her sexual history to her new suitor, then he married her and discovered she is not a virgin. Not telling her betrothed is a serious violation. It is the same thing Joseph erroneously thought Mary was guilty of in Matthew 1:18-25.

She also effectively stole the cost difference between the virgin-equivalent bride-price and the non-virgin-equivalent bride price from her husband. The man who took her virginity should have paid the virgin-equivalent bride-price (and either did or did not), and her husband should have paid a bride-price equivalent to a non-virgin. (In other words, using simple numbers in US dollars, if the bride price for a virgin is $15,000 and the bride price for a non-virgin is $5,000, the fiancé should have paid her father $5,000 but instead paid $15,000, representing a theft of $10,000.) But what, exactly, is the sin that triggers this death sentence?

There are a couple of words in verse 21 to study in the Hebrew, in particular the words translated as the following phrases in the NASB: "disgraceful sin," "playing the prostitute," and "evil."

<u>Disgraceful sin</u>
https://biblehub.com/hebrew/5039.htm

Definition

nebalah: Folly, foolishness, disgrace, senselessness

1. foolishness, i.e. (morally) wickedness
2. concretely, a crime
3. by extension, punishment

<u>Playing the prostitute</u>

https://biblehub.com/hebrew/liznot_2181.htm

https://www.studylight.org/lexicons/eng/hebrew/2181.html

Definition

1. to commit fornication, be a harlot, play the harlot
    a. (Qal)
        i. to be a harlot, act as a harlot, commit fornication
        ii. to commit adultery
        iii. to be a cult prostitute
        iv. to be unfaithful (to God) (figuratively)
    b. (Pual) to play the harlot
    c. (Hiphil)
        i. to cause to commit adultery
        ii. to force into prostitution
        iii. to commit fornication

<u>Evil</u>

https://biblehub.com/hebrew/hara_7451.htm

https://www.studylight.org/lexicons/eng/hebrew/
7451.html

Definition
1. adj
     a. bad, evil
          i. bad, disagreeable, malignant
          ii. bad, unpleasant, evil (giving pain,
               unhappiness, misery)
          iii. evil, displeasing
          iv. bad (of its kind-land, water, etc.)
          v. bad (of value)
          vi. worse than, worst (comparison)
          vii. sad, unhappy
          viii. evil (hurtful)
          ix. bad, unkind (vicious in disposition)
          x. bad, evil, wicked (ethically)
               1. in general, of persons, of
                    thoughts
               2. deeds, actions
2. n m
     a. evil, distress, misery, injury, calamity
          i. evil, distress, adversity
          ii. evil, injury, wrong
          iii. evil (ethical)
3. n f
     a. evil, misery, distress, injury
          i. evil, misery, distress
          ii. evil, injury, wrong

### iii. evil (ethical)

Deuteronomy 22:21

*then they shall bring the girl out to the doorway of her father's house, and the men of her city shall stone her to death, because she has committed a disgraceful sin in Israel by playing the prostitute in her father's house; so you shall eliminate the evil from among you.*

There does seem to be some significance of the fact that Moses mentioned she has done this in her father's house, and that she is to be executed at the doorway of her father's house. This verse does not suggest he is aware of her non-virgin status. So, in a sense she would have been undercutting him with her deception. The father is the head of the house and presumably prior to her engagement (and perhaps as part of the activity leading up to it) he was speaking to others regarding his daughter and her sexual status. So, for him to describe her as a virgin, receive a bride-price appropriate for a virgin, and then the husband discovers and publicly proves that she is not a virgin to the point that the elders of the city are involved, his reputation would presumably be seriously damaged. Were this sort of thing to become widespread, then no household would have any credibility.

Considering the Hebrew words just reviewed, it is senseless, disgraceful, immoral, profane and is an act somewhere between adultery and prostitution for a non-virgin woman to marry a man by deceiving him to think she is a virgin when in reality she is not...and he will realize she isn't only after the ceremony is over, after he has paid the father a bride price for virgins. It appears that the sin was not in the premarital sex, but in the deception regarding its occurrence. And in particular the economic and societal consequences of that deception. The consequences are so severe that she – and any other woman who does this – must be executed. Given that there was no punishment at all for the woman in Exodus 22:16,17 (who also engaged in premarital sex), this is not about the prior sex. This passage cannot be interpreted to mean a prohibition on premarital sex. Here, deception is central and is being used to steal potentially substantial amounts of money. Porenia can be claimed in this case because both lying and stealing are involved, both violations of scripture.

### *Deuteronomy 24:1-4*

I have never seen this passage cited in any discussion on premarital sex (or sex in general), but upon discovering it I felt it was worthy of analysis, just to ensure I am not missing anything.

> *When a man takes a wife and marries her, and it happens, if she finds no favor in his eyes because he has found some indecency in her, that he writes her a certificate of divorce, puts it in her hand, and sends*

*her away from his house, and she leaves his house
and goes and becomes another man's wife, and the
latter husband turns against her, writes her a certificate of divorce and puts it in her hand, and sends her
away from his house, or if the latter husband who
took her to be his wife dies, then her former husband
who sent her away is not allowed to take her again to
be his wife, after she has been defiled; for that is an
abomination before the Lord, and you shall not bring
sin on the land which the Lord your God is giving you
as an inheritance.*

Why can't the original man remarry the woman,
what does the passage mean by indecency, and why is
she defiled? Is this passage implying anything about
the nature of sex that is relevant to premarital sex?
This is the concern I was motivated to investigate, but
there is no indication that this is the case. Technically
speaking, there is no direct mention of sex whatso-
ever in this passage. (Clearly, given that two marriages
have occurred, sex is present, but it is not explicitly
mentioned.) What is in play here are regulations on
marriage. This is the passage the Pharisees were challenging Jesus on in Matthew 19:3-9 when they asked
Him about divorce.

The Hebrew word translated here as "indecency"
is actually ervah, which Strong's Hebrew translates as
nakedness. It is used throughout the Old Testament.
It is sometimes rendered in English literally as nakedness, such as Genesis 9:22 "Ham, the father of Canaan,

saw the nakedness of his father, and told his two brothers outside." It is sometimes used as what appears to be a metaphor for sex, for instance, throughout most of Leviticus 18. As an example, Leviticus 18:15, "You shall not uncover the nakedness of your daughter-in-law." The common thread is that ervah is implying something has been revealed. The first husband has learned something about her that causes him to divorce.

The second husband "turns against her." Here, the Hebrew strikes me as especially harsh. The Hebrew word used in Deuteronomy 24 is ūśənê'āh, a specific instance of the Hebrew word Strong's Hebrew lists as "sane" and translates as hate. So, after taking the time to marry this woman, the second husband now hates her to the point that he divorces her. There is also the case where the second husband didn't hate her, but simply died on her. In either case, the first husband cannot remarry her. The reason given in Deuteronomy 24:4 is she has been "defiled." The Hebrew for defiled is huṭṭammā'āh, which appears to be a form of "tame" which means "to be or become unclean."

This is somewhat confusing to me. How did the woman become unclean? Was it the act of the first husband divorcing her? It seems it is probably not the second husband because while he may have also sent her away, he may have simply died. It doesn't seem reasonable that it is because she had sex with the second husband. After all, she presumably had sex with

the first husband and that didn't render her unclean
and therefore unable to marry the second one.  Further,
there is nothing forbidding her from going on to marry
three, four, five, six or more times as long as none of
them are a former original husband.  So, it is not about
having had sex with someone else.  Is she unclean because of whatever she did that the first husband (and
in some cases the second husband) discovered?  These
are questions for which I only have conjecture.  I don't
see a clear answer in scripture.  The only clear obser-
vation I can make is that she cannot go back to the
one who first rejected her.  I could see that kind of
stipulation making certain forms of abuse more difficult to commit, where a man might send a woman away
to punish her and then bring her back in a way that
enables him to dominate her, especially if the second
husband was complicit.

There is also a question as to whether it is possible
for a Christian woman to be defiled.

Acts 10:9-15, 28 comes to mind here.

> *On the next day, as they were on their way and ap-
> proaching the city, Peter went up on the housetop
> about the sixth hour to pray. But he became hungry
> and wanted to eat; but while they were making
> preparations, he fell into a trance; and he saw the
> sky opened up, and an object like a great sheet com-
> ing down, lowered by four corners to the ground, 12
> and on it were all kinds of four-footed animals and
> crawling creatures of the earth and birds of the sky.*

*A voice came to him, "Get up, Peter, kill and eat!" But Peter said, "By no means, Lord, for I have never eaten anything unholy and unclean." Again a voice came to him a second time, "What God has cleansed, no longer consider unholy." ... And he said to them, "You yourselves know that it is forbidden for a Jewish man to associate with or visit a foreigner; and yet God has shown me that I am not to call any person unholy or unclean."*

Similarly, Hebrews 9:13, 14, 22, 24-26

*For if the blood of goats and bulls, and the ashes of a heifer sprinkling those who have been defiled, sanctify for the cleansing of the flesh, how much more will the blood of Christ, who through the eternal Spirit offered Himself without blemish to God, cleanse your conscience from dead works to serve the living God?...And almost all things are cleansed with blood, according to the Law, and without the shedding of blood there is no forgiveness...For Christ did not enter a holy place made by hands, a mere copy of the true one, but into heaven itself, now to appear in the presence of God for us; nor was it that He would offer Himself often, as the high priest enters the Holy Place year by year with blood that is not his own. Otherwise, He would have needed to suffer often since the foundation of the world; but now once at the consummation of the ages He has been revealed to put away sin by the sacrifice of Himself.*

Given what Acts and Hebrews say about Christ's cleansing of us, regardless of how the woman has become huṭṭammā'āh, a person who has received Christ as savior has been cleansed from all forms of uncleanness. While I still have open questions about Deuteronomy 24:1-4, I do not see anything here that has a bearing on the question of premarital sex.

*Matthew 5:28*

Before concluding this section, it would be valuable to consider the word lust, as sex is not often discussed in our culture without the word lust somewhere entering the conversation. And of course, Jesus had some serious words to say about lust:

> *but I say to you that everyone who looks at a woman with lust for her has already committed adultery with her in his heart.*

What does this mean? I was effectively taught (not so much with words as with attitudes) that this scripture means if a guy looks at a woman and becomes aroused then he is lusting. Basically, if you get an erection you've sinned.

Fortunately, that teaching is based on an inaccurate definition of lust. The false teaching essentially defined lust as sexual excitement, which is utterly bogus. Let us gain a better understanding by first examining the context in which the word lust occurs, then move to Greek definitions of the two words used in the New Testament for lust, and then develop a practical, operational understanding of lust. From the beginning, we should note that the word lust is not a sexual term. Lust is a general activity. One might lust for money. One might lust for power. One might lust for free time. One might lust for sex. Sex is merely one of a virtually unlimited number of targets for lust.

One of the more general discussions of lust is James 4:1,2.

*What is the source of quarrels and conflicts among you? Is the source not your pleasures that wage war in your body's parts? You lust and do not have, so you commit murder. And you are envious and cannot obtain, so you fight and quarrel. You do not have because you do not ask.*

James 1:14,15 also says:

*But each one is tempted when he is carried away and enticed by his own lust. Then when lust has conceived, it gives birth to sin; and sin, when it has run its course, brings forth death.*

The general context in these scriptures indicates that lust involves a taking of something that you do not have the right to have. It is born in a frame of mind that says, "me first, at the expense of whatever gets in my way." As a guiding principle, lust comes from the framework that places self at the center and makes the primary goal the obtaining of what you want with a willingness to do any wrongs it takes to get what you want. The problem is not so much the wanting, as it is the wanting at any cost. In a sense it is a form of idolatry because the will to satisfy your desire occupies the place in your heart that the will to do God's will should occupy.

Fortunately, in addition to context, we can also examine definitions. The English word lust is translated from two similar Greek words that are used in the New Testament: epithumia, the more specific term, and epithumeo, the more general term which is sometimes translated as lust and sometimes translated as desire, depending on the context. My bible has a Hebrew and Greek dictionary for certain words, including these two. Epithumia is defined as "a longing (especially for what is forbidden); the active and individual desire resulting from pathos, the diseased condition of the soul." The more general epithumeo is defined, "to set the heart upon, i.e., long for (rightfully or otherwise); to have the affections directed toward anything; desire; long after; to desire in a good sense; to desire or long for as a matter of natural course; to desire in a bad sense as coveting and lusting after."

Much like pornea, epithumeo becomes lustful sin and not legitimate desire where the desire is either for something forbidden or is packaged in a willingness to utilize methods that are forbidden in scripture. The desire is overriding your commitment to God. Sexual desires should be considered in this context to determine whether they are lust or not. If these desires are acted out in real life, would anything take place that is forbidden in scripture? However, the original question of whether premarital sex is forbidden in the Bible remains unanswered by this verse. (If verses can be found to show that it is forbidden, then any desire for it would by definition then be lust. But if not, then the desire does not automatically equal lust.)

# Chapter 6

# Actual Prohibitions

We have now firmly explored my dilemma. A deeper examination of the scriptures used as backdrops when preaching not to have premarital sex has revealed those scriptures do not say to not have premarital sex. This does not mean that there are no prohibitions in the Bible, only that the scriptures commonly used to justify a pre-determined conclusion did not support that conclusion. So, where are any prohibitions in the Bible and what do they say?

Chapters 18 and 20 of the Book of Leviticus (and to a lesser extent Leviticus 19:20-22) do go into rigorous detail identifying various sexual sins and listing various forbidden sexual unions. Given that the Pentateuch defined the law for the people of Israel, it is unlikely that there could exist a sexual prohibition that is not found in these books (though I continue to look for any elsewhere). The prohibitions listed are very precise, forbidding a man to "uncover the nakedness of" (I assume this means to mean have sex with): any blood relative, your mother, your father's wife, your sister, your granddaughter, your aunt, your daughter-in-law, your brother's wife, a woman and her daughter, a woman and her granddaughter, a woman during her "menstrual impurity", your neighbor's wife, another man's wife, a male, or an animal. Additionally, a man may not marry a woman and her sister while the woman is alive. And while obviously not relevant in today's world, a man may not have sexual relations with a female slave acquired for another man. As an aside, Numbers 5:11-31 indicates it is a sin for a married woman to unfaithfully have sexual relations with another man and hide it from her husband.

<u>Forbidden Sexual Practices</u>
Leviticus 18 – "uncover the nakedness of" phrase; assuming to mean have sex with

| | |
|---|---|
| 18:6 | Any blood relative |
| 18:7 | Your mother |
| 18:8 | Your father's wife |
| 18:9 | Your sister |
| 18:10,11 | Your granddaughter |
| 18:12-14 | Your aunt |
| 18:15 | Your daughter-in-law |
| 18:16 | Your brother's wife |
| 18:17 | A woman and her daughter |

18:17                        A woman and her granddaughter

18:18                        May not marry a woman and her sister while the woman is alive

18:19                        A woman during her "menstrual impurity"

18:20                        Your neighbor's wife

18:22                        A male

18:23                        An animal

Deuteronomy 22

22:13-19                  Falsely accuse new wife of not being a virgin

22:20,21                  Woman falsely portraying self as virgin to new husband

22:22                        Sex with a married woman

22:23,24                  Consensual sex with a virgin woman engaged to someone else

22:25-27                  Rape of a virgin woman engaged to someone else

22:30                        His father's wife


<u>Punishments for Sexual Violations (Note: punishment for the woman is identical to that of the man)</u>

Leviticus

19:20                        A female slave acquired for another man

20:10                        Another man's wife

20:11                        His father's wife

20:12                        His daughter-in-law

20:13                          A male
20:14                          Marries woman and her mother
20:15,16                       An animal
20:17                          His sister, his father's daugh-ter, or his mother's daughter
20:18                          A menstruous woman
20:19                          His mother's sister or his fa-ther's sister
20:20                          His uncle's wife
20:21                          His brother's wife


<u>Non-punishment consequences of a sexual act</u>
Deuteronomy 22:28,29        If have sex with a non-engaged virgin, must marry and cannot ever divorce her

So far, and this is what was the surprise to me, there is no mention of consensual sex with an unmarried, non-engaged, non-relative, non-virgin female. There is a tremendous amount of detail in Leviticus 18, 19, 20, and Deuteronomy 22, yet this is not mentioned here. There is also a significant level of detail in Leviticus 15:16-18 and Deuteronomy 23:10. Both passages discuss emissions of semen, which as written would be inclusive both that resulting from wet dreams and from physical contact with a woman. It is described as unclean requiring washing and in the case of a military encampment against the enemies of Israel, the man with the emission must go outside the camp and remain there until sunset. But it is not called sin, which of course it could not, because as written it would include emissions of semen resulting from husband-and-wife interaction and it is blatantly obvious that cannot be sin. It appears it would only be sin if it resulted from the contacts forbidden in Leviticus 18-20 and Deuteronomy 22. Leviticus and Deuteronomy legislate sexual limits with a high degree of precision. I looked within these comprehensive regulations to find prohibitions on unmarried, non-engaged, non-relative sex with non-virgin females, but they are not present. And unless I missed something, they are not anywhere else in the Bible.

Leviticus 18-20 and Deuteronomy 22 appear to be the core of every scripture in the rest of the Bible that talks about sexual sins. Every scripture I have found elsewhere that clearly forbids a specific sexual act is referencing an act forbidden in these scriptures. If there are no scriptures that prohibit additional sexual acts, then fornication/sexual immorality is limited to the committing of one or more of these forbidden acts, or violating other scriptures in the process of committing otherwise unforbidden acts. As an easily obvious example, lying to your spouse in order to have sex would be immoral because it violates the commandment in Ephesians 4:25 (among others) to speak the truth; therefore, it would be sexual immorality.

What am I missing? The Christian church teaches that sexual intercourse between two unmarried people is fornication and therefore a sin. I do not see that teaching in the Bible. Where is it?

# Chapter 7

# Consideration for Others

Even if there are no commandments that specifi-cally prohibit an unmarried man from having sex there are definitely other Biblical guidelines. One of the first that jumps to mind is I Corinthians 6:12.

*All things are permitted for me, but not all things are of benefit. All things are permitted for me, but I will not be mastered by anything.*

The absence of a prohibition does not equal the provision of carte blanche. One of the highest consid-erations is the second greatest commandment, which is listed in the Bible in several places:

Leviticus 19:11-18

*'You shall not steal, nor deal falsely, nor lie to one another. And you shall not swear falsely by My name, so as to profane the name of your God; I am the Lord. 'You shall not oppress your neighbor, nor rob him. The wages of a hired worker are not to re-*

*main with you all night until morning. You shall not curse a person who is deaf, nor put a stumbling block before a person who is blind, but you shall revere your God; I am the Lord. 'You shall not do injustice in judgment; you shall not show partiality to the poor nor give preference to the great, but you are to judge your neighbor fairly. You shall not go about as a slanderer among your people; and you are not to jeopardize the life of your neighbor. I am the Lord. 'You shall not hate your fellow countryman in your heart; you may certainly rebuke your neighbor, but you are not to incur sin because of him. You shall not take vengeance, nor hold any grudge against the sons of your people, <u>but you shall love your neighbor as yourself</u>; I am the Lord.*

## Matthew 22:35-40

*And one of them, a lawyer, asked Him a question, testing Him: "Teacher, which is the great commandment in the Law?" And He said to him, "'You shall love the Lord your God with all your heart, and with all your soul, and with all your mind.' This is the great and foremost commandment. The second is like it, 'You shall love your neighbor as yourself.' Upon these two commandments hang the whole Law and the Prophets."*

## Matthew 7:12

*In everything, therefore, treat people the same way you want them to treat you, for this is the Law and the Prophets.*

## Mark 12:28-31

*One of the scribes came up and heard them arguing, and recognizing that He had answered them well, asked Him, "What commandment is the foremost of all?" Jesus answered, "The foremost is, 'Hear, Israel! The Lord is our God, the Lord is one; and you shall love the Lord your God with all your heart, and with all your soul, and with all your mind, and with all your strength.' The second is this: 'You shall love your neighbor as yourself.' There is no other commandment greater than these."*

## Romans 13:8-10

*Owe nothing to anyone except to love one another; for the one who loves his neighbor has fulfilled the Law. For this, "You shall not commit adultery, You shall not murder, You shall not steal, You shall not covet," and if there is any other commandment, it is summed up in this saying, "You shall love your neighbor as yourself." Love does no wrong to a neighbor; therefore love is the fulfillment of the Law.*

## I Corinthians 13:4-7

*Love is patient, love is kind, it is not jealous; love does not brag, it is not arrogant. It does not act disgracefully, it does not seek its own benefit; it is not provoked, does not keep an account of a wrong suffered, it does not rejoice in unrighteousness, but rejoices with the truth; it keeps every confidence, it believes all things, hopes all things, endures all things.*

Philippians 2:4

> *Do not merely look out for your own personal interests, but also for the interests of others.*

I John 3:17

> *But whoever has worldly goods and sees his brother or sister in need, and closes his heart against him, how does the love of God remain in him?*

These verses govern all of life, including any decision to have or not have sex. In the presence or absence of any other guidance, consider these verses as the framework to decide whether or not to have sex. Up until now I've talked about this generally from a perspective generally centered on me – how to identify what God has or has not restricted and subordinating my desires to that. But as these verses indicate, it is equally important to consider what the implications are for others? How does a decision to have or not have sex affect the person you might have sex with, as well as other parties?

I have a suspicion that sex has a magnifying effect on any goodness or sin that accompanies it. There is only a light scriptural correlation to suggest this in Proverbs 30:18,19

> *There are three things which are too wonderful for me, four which I do not understand: the way of the eagle in the sky, the way of a snake on a rock, the way of a ship in the middle of the sea, and the way of a man with a virgin.*

As this verse implies, it is also obvious in all facets of life that sex has a powerful impact and has had one throughout human experience. Thus, I suspect, for instance, that a lie told in conjunction with sex has a more damaging impact that that same lie told without being accompanied by sex. I don't definitively know this to be true, but it is a strong suspicion and it might indicate why pornea (sexual immorality) is specifically called out as opposed to the individual sexual sins listed in Leviticus and Deuteronomy. (Pornea encapsulates not just the forbidden acts, but even non-forbidden acts if done in forbidden ways.)

# Chapter 8

# Biblical Responsibility to Truth

I Timothy 2:15

*Be diligent to present yourself approved to God as a worker who does not need to be ashamed, accurately handling the word of truth.*

Proverbs 11:14

*Where there is no guidance the people fall, but in an abundance of counselors there is victory.*

Proverbs 15:20-22

*A wise son makes a father glad, but a foolish man despises his mother. Foolishness is joy to one who lacks sense, but a person of understanding walks straight. Without consultation, plans are frustrated, but with many counselors they succeed.*

The central premise that was the foundation for my early development and the cornerstone of my sexual theology appears to have been shown to be false. The Western, modern colloquial definition of fornication to mean sex between people not married to each other is not an accurate representation of the Greek word pornea. I realized this about a decade ago, but allowed myself to be paralyzed from studying the matter further, because the church already has a position and reaching any other conclusion is a scary thing. But Christianity is not about following the words of humans. It is about following the Word of God.

As Christians, we have an obligation to seek the truth and to understand the Word of God ourselves. It is worth noting that a bad definition does not necessarily mean that the initial conclusion was incorrect, but it does not mean it was correct either. It simply means that additional information is needed to reach ANY conclusion. What I have learned in this study will affect not only me, but an unknown number of others, so this is, to borrow a certain organization's saying, a serious matter. And with the above scriptures in mind, I did seek the counsel of others.

# Chapter 9

# Experiences of Others

The wisdom and experiences of others are not scripture, but they can add additional perspectives and context, which is helpful in light of I Corinthians 6:12 – *"All things are permitted for me, but not all things are of benefit. All things are permitted for me, but I will not be mastered by anything."* I will share some things others shared with me, but out of respect for their privacy I will not share all details or provide any identifying information. I contacted a number of Christians I know well. Some are actively involved in Christian ministry, others are not. But all received a significant amount of biblical discipleship training. Their responses follow. Where I needed to delete words from the middle of a phrase to protect anonymity the deleted words or phrases are marked in {brackets}.

## Perspective 1

{NUMBER DELETED} opinions is a lot of voices to sift through.  Be careful. Hope everything is well.

## Perspective 2

What you share is valid, but truly poses a conundrum of challenges for single Christians who desire to please God in their lives concerning sex, fornication and what God's word says about it concerning the choices we make with those whom we encounter that want to honor God.

You have delved in and dissected valid scripture in many specific ways reminding me of many things I knew from scripture and revealing all the unknown "non-specifics" that understandably would cause you to question if all the "wait" has been in vain.

Since I am not a virgin, but have been practicing celibacy for over a couple of decades, I think about all the times I "could" have had sex but I was not in a committed relationship. It was more "fleshy" and that's why I took many passes over the years. I do believe in being Soul Tied and that's a lot to get a loose from.

I was listening to an Audible of Devon Franklin's "It Takes A Woman" earlier today while driving from {DELETED} back home to {DELETED}. He discussed sex from a man's and woman's point of view using personal testimonials from good mother and great-aunt. There's much to unpack...Praying for you to hear from the Holy Spirit and that you have peace until clarity and conformation come.

## Perspective 3

There is so much here.  Thank you for sharing.  I will give it some thought and write back.  But I would like to commend you for your tenacity in pursuing God in these troubled times.  If nothing else, I know that God appreciates your heart turned towards Heaven and your desire to see God's will done in your life.

I spoke with a colleague the other week at a conference, telling her about your question and asking if she had any insights.  She teaches a course at {DELETED} on sex and marriage in the Bible, or something to that effect, so I thought she might be helpful.  She followed up with me this week with an email.  I asked if I could share it with you and she said yes.  Please read it below.  There are some reading suggestions embedded.  I'll follow up with another colleague as classes are coming to an end.  I hope you find {DELETED}'s email and her reading suggestions helpful...

This is a tricky question, and a very good one. I'm having a hard time thinking of something appropriate. Most of the more liberal leaning scholarship on this topic has moved away from the question of sex outside of marriage (which I imagine they consider to be a moot point) and focuses instead on LGBTQ sex, which isn't really helpful for your friend. More conservative scholars who are interested in the question seem more likely to reinforce the older interpretations in support of the teaching not to have sex outside of marriage.

In my opinion, these older interpretations don't have a strong understanding of Paul's writing on the subject. Instead of being concerned about sex before marriage, Paul wanted to convey that believers should limit having sex altogether—that is, even married people would do well to refrain from having sex. Paul knew being celibate wasn't for everyone, but he does see it as the ideal. Being able to restrain sexual passion was something ancient people understood as very difficult to do, but it was also a sign of virtue and philosophical or religious achievement.

What we do with Paul's message is another question altogether. In Paul's context, there were lots of reasons why this teaching made sense to people. It corresponded to what they already thought of as virtue. But it doesn't really work in the same way for our context—if it did, conservative Christians wouldn't be teaching "love waits," they'd be teaching kids not to have sex at all. However, for your friend, who has already spent a good number of years devoting his life to God in this way, it may be comforting to know that ancient Christians absolutely thought that living a chaste life was virtuous and that it brought you closer to God.

For an interpretation of Paul along the lines of what I'm indicating here, see Dale Martin, "Paul without Passion", chapter 5 of Sex and the Single Savior: Gender and Sexuality in Biblical Interpretation (Louisville:

Westminster John Knox, 2006). And for a fuller explo-ration of chastity as an early Christian virtue, Peter Brown's classic The Body and Society: Men, Women, and Sexual Renunciation in Early Christianity (New York: Columbia University Press, 1988) is still very good—a bit dated in parts, but maybe not the parts that would matter to your friend. These are both pretty academic books. I hope that's okay.

I hope that helps! If I think of anything else, I'll let you know.


## Perspective 4

Thank you for this question. I hope my response helps.

First, I believe you said scripture will be the only de-termining factor in your decision making.

If that is true, you have your answer in I Corinthians 7:1-2.

> *"Now concerning the things about which you wrote, it is good for a man not to touch a woman. But because of sexual immoralities, each man is to have his own wife, and each woman is to have her own husband."*

1 Corinthians 7:1-2 NASB2020

I am assuming (brilliant man that you are) you are fa-miliar with the term hermeneutics.

It is the only way by which scripture should be eval-uated. I will leave it to you to apply hermeneutics to this passage.

{PERSONAL INFORMATION DELETED}

The moment sex is introduced into a relationship, it is the ultimate "defrauding" because it means I have taken the area God meant for marriage and allowed it to become a determining factor in the development of our relationship.

What is sexual oneness? Why is it the pinnacle of a relationship with a woman? God ordained sex for marriage because He knew it is the ultimate act of oneness, vulnerability, intimacy, transparency... etc. etc. etc.

I have not had sexual vaginal intercourse with anyone outside of my marriage. {PERSONAL INFORMATION DELETED} I am sure that if I did it would ruin my relationship with the woman, and {SPOUSE NAME DELETED}, because it then provides a oneness that I cannot fulfill. {PERSONAL INFORMATION DELETED}

I want to continue the dialogue by hearing your thoughts. I am sure you know by now that it is the "wound" (and we all have a wound, courtesy of Adam) I have dealt with the most in my life. Let's talk again.

In Christ's love and mine.


## Perspective 5

I realize that this conversation is sporadic, but here are some of my thoughts from April 2018:

The terms "sexual immorality," "fornication," and "adultery" when used from a Biblical perspective all include in the basic definition sexual intimacy between a man and woman who are not "married" to each other.

Therefore, the first question seems to be, "What is marriage?" The basic definition is not founded upon monogamy because the Samaritan woman at the well was in a monogamous relationship that was not approved by Jesus (St. John 4:4-26) who said that the man was not her "husband," and several Old Testament men had multiple "wives" (David and Jacob, among others). The definition also doesn't seem to include living together because some men who had multiple wives also had concubines who were sexually exclusive to them (tended by deliberately castrated eunuchs) and lived in their homes but were distinguished from their wives (). Also, the definition must consider that a man and woman are considered married unless a "certificate of divorce" has been issued (Deuteronomy 24:1-4, Matthew 5:31-32, 19:3-9; Mark 10:2-12). So, the question stands, if standing before the LORD and He asked, "Where does the Bible support monogamy as the definition of marriage or exclude a certificate of marriage as established by the laws of the land from ancient to modern times (Romans 13:1-2)?" What would you say?

Please do share a follow up document with any new insights that you're considering.

## Perspective 6

Sex is not wrong in wedlock or out of wedlock. Do whatever you want to do.

## Perspective 7

[NO RESPONSE RECEIVED TO REQUEST TO FRIEND FOR PERMISSION TO INCLUDE. The perspective did not include any additional scriptures or insights.]

## Perspective 8

I wanted to follow up with my response to your email. First, thank you so much for sharing your heart with me, especially on a topic that is very personal. Secondly, as I read your letter, I sensed a little frustration mixed with an earnest pursuit to understand the real truth of the matter regarding premarital sex.

Here are my thoughts for you to consider:

God is bigger than the Bible.

The answer you seek can only be answered by the Holy Spirit who lives inside of you.

I believe your real question is not about sex, or premarital sex, or what you're NOT allowed to do as a Christian. But rather, I believe your question is Why am I not married by now, especially when I have been obedient to God's word?

Sex is natural and necessary for human life. Period. But when sex becomes an idol and a distraction that slows us down from becoming the best version of what God created us to be, that's when sex becomes a sin. And there are always consequences or negative repercussions to sin (perversion, damaged relationships, unwanted pregnancies, a broken consciousness, low self-esteem, STDs, etc.). So rather than debate on the "what" not to do according to the Bible, I pull up and look for the "why" and seek the wisdom behind it.

On a side note, I think religion is loud about the things we shouldn't do and quiet on the main thing we should do.

Ultimately, I've concluded God wants us to become the best representation and manifestation of His big idea for us—to have dominion/rulership over the Earth in the likeness of how God has rulership in Heaven. Earth is, or should be, an extension or a "colony" of the Kingdom of Heaven. That's the main thing. Any act that thwarts that vision is sin. So, sex that's out-of-order—and other vices like drunkenness, gluttony, slothfulness, pride, etc.—can derail and even destroy us from achieving God's big idea for us.

The scripture I have for you is this: Delight yourself in the Lord, and He will give you the desires of your heart. – Psalm 37:4

The word delight means "that which gives a high degree of pleasure or satisfaction." Frustration is the opposite of delight.

I don't believe God would put a desire in your heart and not fulfill it, including your desire for sex in a manner that is decent and in order—i.e., marriage, where the marriage bed is undefiled. King David was a man who engaged in fornication, no matter how you define it. But he was still God's anointed and remained a king with God's favor even after he committed fornicated acts.

And so, be encouraged. You have to find your wife. She is out there. And perhaps there are some areas in your life that God wants to develop so that you are ready for the woman, or type of woman, you choose to pursue.

I hope this helps. You are not average; if you were looking for average, then the pool of women would be plentiful. But because you are kingly, you have to be a little more diligent and patient because true queens are few and far between. But she is out there. ◈

I'll get off my soap dish now. Anyway, I'm glad you're getting close to your answer. I hope all is well with you.  Let me know your thoughts if you have further questions. It's always good to hear from you.

## Perspective 9

The short answer is, your extensive research has led both you & I to the exact same conclusion.

Sex outside of marriage is not equivalent to sexual immorality.

Sex + sin equals sexual immorality — which also could also mean that married people may be engaging in sexual immorality, such forced abstinence, non-consensual sex, abusive sex, sex as a manipulative tool, intentionally mediocre sex, etc.

I was one of the few practicing Christians in seminary, so my Christian peers & I would have frequent &

intense discussions on the differences we were finding between Black religious culture, commonly accepted Eurocentric ideology, the typical assumptions about the Bible and the actual Biblical text.

We often found the best way to avoid hypocrisy, wish-fulfillment, cowardice, mindless conformity & fallacious error is to seek God's guidance via prayer, worship, study & fellowship on a foundation of love, patience, humility & wisdom. Humor, curiosity & kindness are often more important than our digital lexicons & concordances.

Personally, I intend to be sexually active when I meet a man that God has approved as suitable for the life God has called me to live. I will treat sex just as I do many of the other physical pleasures — eating, sleeping, bathing...

I recognize the biological role they play in my life. I avoid both overindulgence & deprivation.

I acknowledge the cultural imprints that have expanded these lifesaving activities to include & represent fellowship, privilege & wealth.

I receive the pleasure these acts nearly always contain as a gift from God; as a Divine reminder to treat them as part of my worshipful daily sacrament; as testament that God is good and His mercy endures to all generations; as witness that truly His rain & sunlight fall on the both just & the unjust.

I can therefore bring my sexuality to my beloved as an act of edification & affirmation, just as I would my cooking, my singing, my household chores or any other righteous-yet-not-necessarily-commanded act of loving kindness. And I do expect the same from him.

I want very much to be in a godly, romantic relationship with a compatible, mutually attracted man. All things work together for good, including my waiting. In due season I will either receive my heart's desire or not. Either way, I will continue reaping the benefits of avoiding the pitfalls & harms of spiritual & romantic incompatibility.

God bless you on your journey.

Jeremiah 33:3 — *Call to Me and I will answer you and show you great and unsearchable things that you did not know.*

Isaiah 30:21 — *Your ears will hear a word behind you saying, "This is the way, walk in it," whenever you turn to the right hand or whenever you turn to the left.*

## Perspective 10

It is good to hear from you. I keep tabs of the wonderful achievements you have made {DELETED}. I am happy for all the Lord as done through you and I know he will continue to you use you as a shining example in all you do.

I thank you again for reaching out to me to discuss this sensitive subject. I understand there is a level of vulnerability in discussing the matter of sex so I will attempt to be as transparent in my reply as possible.

After reading through your letter several times, each time it caused me to pause at a different point and meditate on what I would write.  After prayer and discussion with my wife (although we discussed the topic, know it was in complete anonymity), I feel at peace with what I am supposed to say.

In replying to your questions and discussing the topic of fornication; what the Bible says that it is and is not, I am led to take a little different route that I believe in the end will still bring clarity to your questions.

In discussing the topic of fornication in the perspective of sex, instead of starting with what fornication is/ is not, I would like to start with what sex is and is not in the context of the Bible.

To understand this, we must go back to the beginning.  in biblical studies, there is what it's called the "Law of First Mention." If you are not familiar with it, it basically states that when you want to gain an understanding of a word, topic, etc. In the Bible, you must find where it is first mentioned to build the foundation of your understanding.

This will cause me to go to the book of Genesis, specifically chapters 2,3 and 4.  In Genesis 2:23-25, after God had created Woman, it states:

> *"And Adam said, This is now bone of my bones, and flesh of my flesh: she shall be called Woman, because she was taken out of Man. Therefore, shall a man leave his father and his mother, and shall cleave unto his wife: and they shall be one flesh. And they*

*were both naked, the man and his wife, and were not ashamed."*
Genesis 2:23-25 KJV

A couple of things I would like to point out here. First the process of leaving and cleaving. It implies that the man and woman will leave the parental relationships they had held as primary and be drawn to the relationship he and she will have with each other. The cleaving is not instant, but a process that happens over time as the two become more acquainted with each other. For this relationship to be successful it requires transparency and trust. It requires vulnerability by both parties and a responsibility by both parties to be found trustworthy of that vulnerability. This is why it says in verse 25 that they were *"naked and unashamed."*

When it states in verse 24 that *"the two shall become one flesh,"* I believe that this is more than just a literal sexual union, but an understanding between the husband and wife that they are connected to each other, and what one does ultimately affects the other for the good or bad.

I said all of this to set up what happens next in chapter 3, which is known as the fall of man. We know the struggle that takes place, the temptation and the stress we see on the relationship between God and man, and husband and wife. Yet in spite of what takes place, Adam and Eve still stay together through this. And at a time when they could have been drawn farther apart, you could say their perseverance through this trial brought them closer together. I say this because in Genesis 4:1 the Bible states that... "Adam knew (has sex with) Eve his wife..."

From these passages of scripture, I believe God points out clearly two things that will be valid to our discussion:

1. Sin is disobedience to God (I did not go into detailed explanation of this first point because I know you are more than familiar with the story of the fall).

2. Sex was intended by God to be shared in a persevering, covenant relationship between a husband and wife, and that anything otherwise is disobedience to God.

So, from this foundation, we find many instances in the Bible where man disobeyed God in the sexual relationship. I will for the sake of not being too exhaustive discuss only two: David and Bathsheba, and Amnon and Tamar.

In starting with the latter story, Amnon and Tamar were brother and sister, but Amnon became so obsessed with her that he became sick in love (2 Samuel 13:1-2, NLT). This infatuation caused Amnon to sin and have sex with his sister. It is interesting in this story that Tamar appealed to Amnon to ask the King for him to allow Amnon to have her as his wife but, he refused and proceeded to force himself on her. And after the act his "love" turned to hatred because it was more out of lust than love (v 11-18).

But as terrible as this story is, it pales in comparison to what David did with Bathsheba. Not to mention having her husband killed to try to cover up his act of adultery. But the part I want to focus on is in 2 Samuel 12, when the prophet Nathan confronts David and uncovers his sins. In v.11 Nathan tells David:

*"This is what the Lord says: Because of what you have done, I will cause your own household to rebel against you...(NLT)."*

So not only was David wrong in the act of adultery, but it led him to commit other sins to try to cover it up, and brought a curse on the rest of his family as well, which one could argue lead to the situation with Amnon and Tamar. I bring up these scriptures to make a few more points:

1. Sex outside of the covenant relationship of marriage has consequences, and some can be deadly. Not always literally, but death of relationships, jobs, families, etc.

2. The consequences can not only negatively affect you, but other friendships, relationships, and generations to come.

So having established all of this, let me jump ahead here a bit because I don't want to ignore your thoughts on fornication. By starting with the story of Adam and Eve I wanted to establish what sex is intended to be in the eyes of God. In understanding this we also understand that anything else outside of this goes against his intentions, which is disobedience, and ultimately sin.

We could go back and forth to debate the meaning of fornication, but I believe in spite of what fornication may, or may not include in its definition of unlawful sex, the Bible's original definition of sex makes it plain what is lawful/unlawful to God.  Similarly, I hope my examples of the consequences of unlawful sexual relations help to further substantiate this point.

However, before I conclude this, I must cite one more passage of scripture.  In 1 Corinthians 7:1-9:

> *"But because there is so much sexual immorality, each man should have his own wife, and each woman should have her own husband. The husband should fulfill his wife's sexual needs, and the wife should fulfill her husband's needs. The wife gives authority over her body to her husband, and the husband gives authority over his body to his wife. Do not deprive each other of sexual relations, unless you both agree to refrain from sexual intimacy for a limited time so you can give yourselves more completely to prayer. Afterward, you should come together again so that Satan won't be able to tempt you because of your lack of self-control. But I wish everyone were single, just as I am. Yet each person has a special gift from God, of one kind or another. So, I say to those who aren't married and to widows—it's better to stay unmarried, just as I am. But if they can't control themselves, they should go ahead*

*and marry. It's better to marry than to burn with lust."*

1 Corinthians 7:2-5, 7-9 NLT

To me this solidifies my previous statements about God's design for sexual relations. Paul only gives us two options when it comes to having sex: either abstain like me or get married and have all the sex you want.

Let me conclude by saying I admire your self-control and obedience. I truly believe that although you may have felt disillusioned by what you had been taught previously, because of your obedience God has blessed you in other ways. I pray that if it's still your heart's desire to be married that God will send you a wife suitable for you. But if not, I also pray that he will continue to give you the power to observe self-control and to abstain from sex. I say this not just as a friend, but as one who has experienced the joys of sex in marriage, and the consequences of sex outside of marriage.

I wish I could have had the amount of self-control as you. But because I didn't, although my wife and I have a healthy relationship, there are consequences of my disobedience that affects both of us. You see my friend, I {CONSEQUENCE DELETED}. I thank God for his grace that {CONCERN DELETED}, but it was tough wondering if I could ever find someone that would love me in spite of {CONSEQUENCE DELETED}. It was tough trying to come up with a way and the words to tell her before we got married of {CONSEQUENCE

DELETED} and wondering if she would still love me if she knew. It's tough at times to put the thoughts of past unlawful sexual relationships behind you. It's tough living with the fact that I had sex with people that weren't my wife because those feelings and thoughts from the past don't always just fade away.

So, my friend, I hope this encourages you and helps you in your thoughts and decisions moving forward. I again thank you for allowing me to comment and share with you. I hope this helps.

## Perspective 11

I have poured over your letter and spent days thinking about its contents. You have done a tremendously great job in your study of the Bible concerning Sex. I have only read and been made aware of these scriptures only. I know of no other ones! Like you, I have been taught since childhood to "avoid fornication/sexual immorality". The actual Greek definition that you described in your letter was not and is not taught. I like you have had my own journey with being disappointed by what has been taught in the church versus what the Bible actually says regarding sex. It too affected me throughout my college, early and middle adult years. I have been married and divorced and in a serious relationship currently. "Sex" is a major issue. For me the "switch" never came on "magically" just because I was married. My ex-spouse too struggled with this very issue and came in the marriage frustrated and bitter over this very topic from his previous marriage and church teachings. We had several theological discussions regarding it for years. We were raised the same and in church and Holy Spirit filled. Your question is theological but the topic of sex goes far beyond just being theological. It is definitely emotional, physical and spiritual.

I have been able to acknowledge God's Word, my upbringing in my home and church and the many people who know and love me; to give myself grace and patience in this area. I have been in counseling for a myriad of issues that I can truly say has been amazing for me. I am a different person at {AGE DELETED} than I was in my early {AGE DELETED}. As you know, "life" is the best teacher (no matter the joys or sorrows). I know that what I resisted from doing did prevent me from a lot of traumas. However, I often question what happiness and freedom did I miss as well. I do know and firmly believe *"And we know that all things together for good to them that love God, to them who are the called according to His purpose."* Romans 8:28. I am at the place where I am supposed to be despite my past. I am a new creature for sure. I will be in prayer for you as you embark on this part of your journey. I pray God gives you the answers and peace that you need to proceed in whatever direction you enter. Thank you for seeking me out during this time and I love you. By the way, I am extremely proud of all of your accomplishments and hold you in the highest esteem!!! Be Blessed!

## Perspective 12

I have read your difficult question and agree it's a lot, more than I can speak to directly right now. However, I will share what is on my heart.

The last {TIME SPAN DELETED} have been challenging for me. I am in a season of re-evaluating everything, including long held beliefs and mindsets, so I genuinely relate to your situation. How much of the way I have lived my life is a result of culture (Christian, US, southern, patriarchy, racial, etc.) and how much is truly the way God wants me to live. What has my creator and Father designed for me?

In my ongoing search, I am learning to really listen to my body, my feelings, the Holy Spirit within me and God's word and Godly counsel. I know one thing for sure: God loves me and is guiding me through this unique experience of my life. It is not exactly what I expected and some parts I didn't want but it is mine to live and make mistakes and get it right and do the best I can. I will continue to pray for you.

# Chapter 10

# Conclusion

This is not a topic where there will be universal agreement within the church. With the best of intentions and the deepest of commitment to God, Christians are on all sides of this issue. And while there can be adverse consequences from sex, there can also be adverse consequences from abstinence. There can also be positive experiences from premarital sex, and there can be positive experiences from abstinence until marriage. And regardless of how marriage is reached, sex will present both wonders and challenges within marriage. There is no answer that "avoids bad things."

I can remember when my virginity was guarded by an impregnable fortress. Hypothetically, the hottest supermodel could have come up to me, dropped her clothes, begged that I have sexual intercourse with her right there, and I would have told her no without the slightest hesitation. Every woman I've dated thus far has experienced that fortress – to the delight of some and to the horror of others. (For many it began with delight because sex wasn't the first thing on my mind – I wasn't the typical male trying to get her to drop their panties, then it shifted to horror when sex was on their minds and I said no. As women in American culture, they were not used to having their sexual advances rejected by men.) In my mind it was as if they were asking me to choose between them and God; effectively (in my mind) they were declaring war on God and asking me to choose sides. In that context they didn't stand a chance of winning me over.

The foundation of that fortress was a false definition of the Greek word pornea, and with the disintegration of that definition the fortress has also been vaporized. That does not mean I'm going to run out and have sex right away (I'm not), only that in the past it was not even a topic of discussion. I'm no longer in that universe.

There is freedom to choose to have sex only after marriage (or even to simply just choose to not have sex today with no implication about whether or not to choose to have sex tomorrow), just as one can choose to be a vegan, or choose to be a doctor, or choose to not drink alcohol. Basically, I have not found any scriptures that indicate it would be a sin for an unmarried man (me) to have sex with an unmarried woman. The non-negotiable absolute I used to live by is gone.

Ultimately, I am open to someone who can prove me wrong; to find the scripture I missed or to show me how I misread a verse and got the wrong meaning. Once, this was out of lack of confidence; how could I possibly be correct if other reputable people disagree? But I know I am an intelligent person and I know this work is sound.  I am confident that I have reached the answer to my questions.  Yet, I am human, so the possibility of my having missed something exists.  So, I am always open to being shown new information.

I deeply appreciate everyone's prayers and inputs. Both are always welcome in my life.  I don't know what the future holds, only that I will continue to look to God and search the scriptures for how I should live.

# ABOUT THE AUTHOR

Solomon Thomas Jacob is a pseudonym, chosen for symbolic relevance. Solomon, of course, famously asked God for wisdom when God offered to give him whatever he wanted. The Apostle Thomas required proof to believe that Jesus rose from the dead. Jacob wrestled all night with an angel of God, refusing to let go until he had received a blessing. I am seeking wisdom by searching the Word of God. And I require proof in the form of Biblical scriptures – the opinions of even spiritual leaders are insufficient for me to believe. I refuse to let go of this quest until I have received God's blessing and the wisdom I seek. Solomon, Thomas, and Jacob. All of these loved God and yet were fallible men. Collectively, they are an appropriate symbolic label for my search for answers.

What little I will reveal of myself is that I am an African American Christian male. I was raised in a God-fearing family and was saved at the age of eight. As of this writing, I have never been married and have never had sexual intercourse. I have been continuously active in church since early childhood and do not see that ever changing. I am not a minister or in any religious profession, though I have been extensively involved in various Bible study communities both inside and outside of formal church structures. I hold multiple academic degrees in a profession unrelated to religious practice and I believe my analytic approach to this topic is perhaps influenced by my academic background; it thus may not be for everyone. But for those it blesses, I am glad.